The Dream of

Albion rose with the dawn to meet the morning
sun spreading its wings of light. His thoughts were
poems and his words were prayers.
Albion thought:

"Of all the mountains of this land,
Love alone touches heaven's hand.
That golden disc over the mountain top
Is like a halo over the blessed rock."

And his flower grew!
He felt himself filled with fresh buds bursting into
bloom - their petals spreading, gently, beautifully.
Albion spoke:

"My daily life is my temple."
And he entered the forest:

"Beautiful creatures
Walk barefoot and naked
In the wet garden
Among the lily and the orchid,
Break not a stem,
Crush not a leaf,
Tread softly
And lie yourselves down

In its peace."

These were Albion's thoughts as he watched his people moving through the spaces in their togetherness. He saw a girl, her eyes shone like two blue lamps, piercing Albion's soul. When he looked back at her she fell to the ground.

Embracing her pain, shuddering deep, she gripped her belly then suddenly burst open and became a single lotus flower. She was gone - she had walked in the shadow of the mountain!

Albion picked her flower and breathed its fragrance. Its petals folded around him and he fell into a dream.

Albion spoke:

"My flesh and blood is the altar from which I make my sacrifice."

Then from the flower blossomed forth a dove, it plucked the words from his lips and flew to the heart of the mountain. Then it dawned on him - he too had walked in the shadow of the mountain!

Albion thought:

"Flow gently brave tears,
  Soothe sweetly my fears,
  For we'll melt with the sun
  When Albion's done."

The Dream of Albion

By

Paul Gerard McDermott

To Silke,
my all time
favourite vicar.
With love,

Paul McDermott

Contents

And his flower grew!

Albion's thoughts melted as he felt himself melting into the fragrance of the flower. Wrapped in its petals he felt like a tiny baby being wrapped in silk, like a grain of sand in an oyster shell.

Albion thought:

"Love is like the grit in an oyster,
  It weaves for me some mystery,
  Some destiny and triumphantly
  Proclaims itself a pearl."

When the fragrance of the flower left him, he found that while he was dreaming he had been walking. He had lost himself in the forest and found himself at the foot of the mountain.

In front of him was an opening in the rock issuing water. He drank the water. It tasted of fire and ran through him like laughter, making a river of his veins until he too became part of the flow.

Albion thought:

"Love will open a grateful vein,
  The cup of joy is filled with pain."

And he entered the mountain!

A tiny pin of light appeared from deep within the belly of the mountain. Albion pushed against the narrowing walls of a long tunnel. The pin of light grew and in a flash came racing down the tunnel, bouncing off the walls and dancing upon the water.

As the light filled the tunnel the living water became his life blood. Then the river began to flood and swept him deep into the heart of the mountain.

In the heart of the mountain was a pool. Albion peered into its depths and to his amazement saw the girl staring back at him. When he looked into her smoking blue eyes he saw his destiny.

Albion spoke:

"Our children are our eternal reward."

And his flower blossomed!

He leaned forward to kiss the girl and plunged to his death. As he was sinking, staring into the two shining blue lamps, Albion thought his last:

"Mystery and destiny -
  The torches of darkness,
  Those flowering dreams
  Blaze their smoking blueness.
  Revealing the gloom
  Of this breathless world,
  They lead me to doom,
  They crown me with pearls."

Daybreak at the dawn of man:

All that lives is born in mist and the mist was bound around Albion's breath. Not with words did he speak but with his first breath, as a newborn child crying for life -

Albion spoke:

"I am."

Butterflies

The paper bag floated, rising up into the air and hovered above the ground drifting aimlessly in the hot sun, caught by a summer breeze that was contained in one small corner where two brick walls met. It spiralled up and down, sometimes moving across and landing again only to pick up once more.

It was beautiful and it mirrored the feeling inside, the feeling that some great power was directing all that has happened and all that was to happen and the electricity in the air suspended her heart like this paper bag and they danced together to the silent music plucked by the hands of God and God was present at this moment, as always and forever more.

The day she met God Charity will always remember, she was three years old and though she knew not who God was, He knew her and that was enough.

At the age of six she found a caterpillar and decided to keep it. She put it in a jar with some leaves and kept it in her bedroom. She nurtured the caterpillar all spring, bringing fresh leaves every other day for the caterpillar's food. It grew fat from love. She cradled it in her hand and with her index finger stroked the fine hairs on its back. It was going to be a butterfly and Charity was fascinated by this. This is why she had kept it because her teacher had told her that caterpillars die and are reborn as butterflies.

The caterpillar crawled and that's how she felt, like a crawling thing in a vast forest but God knew her and though she did not know who God was, He was imprinted on her heart from when she was three.

"Will I be a butterfly one day?" she would ask herself or was she asking the God she did not know? She knew in her heart that one day she would have wings and be able to drift in spirals to the silent music plucked by the hands of God but knowing something in your heart is not the same as knowing something in your head. The things in your head are like bricks or concrete: "Seeing is believing" they say. "I want to feel safe, I want to have friends, I want to have the things I love all around me, I want to be happy."

These are all the things that were in Charity's head but the things in her heart were never realised because finding them was a painful experience. It was like pulling a splinter out of your finger or hauling a heavy shopping bag all the way to the door and holding on, although you can't bear it, until you can put it down. Why you can't put it down halfway I don't know. The answer to that question lies in the heart. None of us can forgive ourselves for failing to reach our goals and that begins at birth but the heart has wings with forgiveness and when you put down the burden without feeling like a failure, the heart stops crawling.

So, Charity was crawling like her caterpillar and she was curious to watch the spectacle of the caterpillar changing into a butterfly to see if it would awaken something in her own heart, something like the moment she had with the paper bag, the moment she met God.

The day came when the caterpillar began to build a cocoon and Charity was there to see it. The caterpillar wove silver threads around itself until it was wrapped in silk and was gone. It hung from a leaf in the jar and was never seen again, only the external shell was left and far from being a disappointment to Charity, it was a release. She had hoped to see the caterpillar die, she was interested to see what the difference was between the living, crawling, hairy caterpillar and its coffin of silk. The point at which it died she was not sure of, now that was a disappointment. She had hoped to see the life leave it and go on to its proper place. She only knew it happened sometime on that day.

Where life goes she could not precisely say but she'd seen it go and that was enough for Charity to wonder what might happen when she died. Where would she go? She started to ask questions and this is when she found out about God:

There was a God in Heaven and He had a son called Jesus, who died and came back to life. There was also a place called Hell and the Devil lived there and a thing called sin, which was bad but because Jesus died it didn't matter about sin, the Devil or Hell.

The day came when the butterfly began to hatch out of the cocoon. Charity saw movement through the transparent shell and took the chrysalis out of the jar. She was sure that this was the moment she would once again meet God but by now she was not sure if God knew her. He seemed so big and she seemed so small in all the time and space in the world. Who was she to Him? Perhaps if she could see Him, He would see her and she would be known to Him and she would find her rightful place in Heaven and so find her rightful place in the world.

The butterfly crawled out of the shell and sat upon Charity's hand with its wings all crumpled and soft. Charity breathed on the butterfly to help its wings to unfold and harden so it could fly. The butterflies wings never opened and it died in her hand. She had interrupted the flow of the paper bag and knocked the wind out of it only to be dragged over the ground never to catch the breeze again. Charity never forgot this moment and to her dying day the greatest burden on her soul was this dead butterfly.

Charity turned sixteen and on her birthday her boyfriend came to her with a very special present. It was a butterfly in a jar, standing very still on a leaf, flexing its wings.

"Why have you brought me this?" asked Charity.

"To prove my love" he said.

"You know you can't keep it in a jar. It is a living thing and belongs in the natural world. You can capture it in a jar but when you do it becomes flightless. It needs to be free and you can catch glimpses of it from time to time." She said.

"That is the nature of love" he said. "Unless it remains out of reach, it dies, like a mystery or a butterfly" and they took the jar into the meadow and unscrewed the lid. Charity did not see a butterfly set free but a paper bag floating in spirals and she understood the need for God to be a mystery.

As a woman Charity had a garden and many flowers grew there. She'd grown to love stillness and saw a side to love that was firm and constant. She grew her garden for many reasons and one of those reasons was for the dead butterfly she once held but she still could not shake off the burden upon her soul.

Well, tragedy struck her life and her loving husband became ill, to the point of death. Cancer they called it and eventually he was put in hospital with no hope of living. She spoke with him many times on his deathbed and on many levels. They remembered when they first cemented their love and set a butterfly free from a jar. They spoke about God:

"Is there a God?" said Charity's husband.

"Yes" said Charity.

"How do you know?"

"I just know."

"How?"

"I don't know how I know, I just know I do."

"And what about Hell?"

"Now that I do know about: If God is the beginning, then God is the end and Hell hath no fury."

"How do you know that?"

"It is what I believe."

"What do you believe?"

"I believe God is a mystery."

"Like love?"

"Or a butterfly."

"I love you and I love the kids."

"We love you too."

"I'm tired of my illness, I'll be glad when it's over."

"You rest now."

He went to sleep with Charity sitting alongside looking out of the window. He never woke up again and before she knew he had died, Charity watched a paper bag dancing upon a summer breeze in the car park and at last, for a fleeting moment, her heart danced once again to the silent music plucked by the hands of God.

The Mosquito

A female mosquito hovered above a stagnant pool of water to lay her eggs. She dropped them one by one into the water - hundreds of them. They were not all going to survive. In fact many of them did not. They were eaten by frogs and other such creatures but the egg we are concerned with is the one hundred and thirty second egg. It had escaped being eaten or destroyed an incalculable number of times.

The time came for it to hatch and out of the egg came a tiny larva not much bigger than a pinhead and not much thicker than a hair. It fed on bacteria in the water, filtering it with tiny hairs. It moulted its shell three or four times until it became a pupa. Even still it should not have survived, many of its brothers and sisters did not but this planet belonged to the one hundred and thirty second egg of one particular mosquito just as much as it belonged to me or you.

Somewhere in another country, far away in the world, there was a man. He was a great man with great ideals, with great words and great opinions. He was also a great sinner. He told of his opinions and the world heard them. They became the dream that awoke in man a new era: One of freedom and unity, one of knowledge and understanding, one of truth and love. His words were written into history and they came to be known as 'The Treatise' and it read like this:

The Treatise

1. Truth and love are a double edged sword - truth slays that which is dying in us and love saves that which is living in us.
2. The heart is clay in the hands of a sculptor - when the material is resistant the sculptor has need to carve truth's likeness and when the material is compliant the sculptor has need to apply love's likeness.
3. The hand of truth lays bare in winter what the face of love blossoms in summer.
4. The tree of life has truth at the root and love in the fruit - when sorrows fall they strengthen the root, bearing fruit of radiant joy.
5. The man who works for love finds meaning in his burden - scratching truth from the earth of love's daily bread.
6. When truth is the source, love is the issue - like a mortal river meeting an eternal ocean.
7. The soul is a ship on the ocean of life - while love fills the sail with passion, truth directs the rudder with reason.

8. Truth is the anchor that gives dominion to love's wings of freedom.
9. As Sun and Moon are celestial bodies closest to the Earth - love gives light to truth and truth reflects love.
10. Truth and love are the pillars of Heaven like man and woman are

   the pillars of the Earth.

One day the great man travelled to a tropical country, the same country as the one hundred and thirty second mosquito. While he was there the mosquito bit him and drank his blood to atone for his sins. He did not feel it at the time but later he felt it itch and he began to scratch it. Days later he had a fever and the great man fell ill with malaria and died. There was mourning and weeping all over the world, for the campaign to which he contributed saw religion safe in the hands of God.

Meanwhile, the one hundred and thirty second mosquito, with the great man's blood in her veins, was laying her eggs in a stagnant pool.

Cups

The dark and the light sat at their table. Upon the table were two cups and a pitcher. The pitcher was poured and the cups were filled. They both drank deep:

Dark: "What is mine and what is yours?"

Light: "Everything that is real is mine and everything that is not is yours."

Dark: "What is real?"

Light: "That which has spirit is real."

Dark: "What is spirit?"

Light: "That which fills this cup is spirit."

Dark: "Does it have spirit if it is empty?"

Light: "If it is empty and yet there is something to fill it, then it has spirit."

Dark: "It only has spirit if there is something to fill it?"

Light: "It is a question of faith."

Dark: "What is faith?"

Light: "faith is an empty cup."

Dark: "What happens to the cup if I break it?"

Light: "Do you not know that He who makes the outside of the cup also makes the   inside?"

Dark: "Flesh for flesh."

Light: "Spirit for spirit."

Dark: "Flesh dies."

Light: "Spirit lives."

Dark: "What is life?"

Light: "Life contains existence."

Dark: "What is existence?"

Light: "To be or not to be, that is the question."

Dark: "What is to be?"

Light: "Everything that has spirit is to be."

Dark: "Am I to be?"

Light: "You are not."

Dark: "So I am nothing?"

Light: "Nothing is the shadow of something."

Dark: "Then I am a shadow?"

Light: "You are everything outside of the light."

Dark: "Then I am everything else?"

Light: "That is how you would have it."

Dark: "Then I am the greater?"

Light: "Life is the greater."

Dark: "Then I am life?"

Light: "You are that which has no life."

Dark: "What portion is there of that which has life and what portion is there of that which has none?"

Light: "There is one portion of that which has life and one portion of that which has none."

Dark: "So we are equal?"

Light: "A shadow has no power because there is no substance in it."

Dark: "so what is mine and what is yours?"

Light: "What you have in your cup is yours and what I have in my cup is   mine."

Dark: "My cup is half empty."

Light:"my cup is half full."

   They both drank deep and emptied their cups then they resumed their positions in the Universe.

Pieces

No.1

War entered the arena disguised as a lion, then peace entered disguised as a lamb. War said:
"I am the poor, the hungry, the blind and the lost."
   Then peace said:
"I am truth and love, the light and the way."
"What is truth?" said war.
   And peace replied:
"Truth is a mountain that is shrouded in mist, though you cannot see it you know it is there because you are climbing it."
"What is love?" said war.
   And peace replied:
"Love is a rose that fills us with joy but if we try to grasp it we find a thorn."
"What is the light?" said war.
   And peace replied:
"The light is a measuring stick by which we calculate everything - if nothing is the conclusion then the measuring stick is wrong."
"What is the way?" said war.
   And peace replied:
"The way is what lies beyond the horizon - tomorrow is full of questions whilst yesterday is full of answers."

Then war said:

"The truth is a blessing to the poor, love satisfies the hungry, the blind can see the light and the lost have found their way."

Then war lay down on the ground and said:

"I surrender."

And the lamb lay down with the lion.

No.2

I was walking in my vineyard and I met a child.
The child asked me:
"Are you Jesus?"
To which I replied:
"No I am John."
Then the child asked:
"But are you the same as Jesus?"
To which I replied:
"No I am the same as John."
Then the child asked:
"But are you Jesus come as John?"
To which I replied:
"No I am come as myself."
Then I asked the child;
"Who are you?"
And the child replied:
"I am Jesus."

No.3

A man went in search of the giver of life. He came to a ruined city and was filled with compassion for the lost kingdom. He realised there was no turning back. He was alone with the elements and was afraid.

His troubled heart led him to the house of a sinner.

He broke bread with him:

"How do you plead?" asked the sinner.

"Guilty" said the traveller.

And his soul was released.

His new found freedom led him to the temple of a saint.

He was offered a cup:

"What is in your cup?" asked the saint.

"My cup is half empty" said the traveller.

"My cup is half full" said the saint.

And he knew where to attach his hope.

This new direction led him to a kingdom that had no end.

He was met by a beggar at the city gate:

"Have you anything to declare?" asked the beggar.

"I come empty handed" said the traveller.

"All begin life as beggars" said the beggar.

And he was allowed to pass.

As with all new citizens he was summoned to the king.

"To what authority do you adhere?" asked the king.
"To the giver of life" said the traveller.
"I am who I am" said the king.
  And he found himself among the living.

Three men were walking from death to life. They came to a river and on the other side was the Kingdom of Heaven.

One man said:

"I have heard say of a bridge over this river."

Another said:

"I too have heard this."

The two men went in search of the bridge, one went up river and the other went down.

Meanwhile, the third man did not believe in the bridge, so he decided to swim across. Halfway across he was drowned.

The man who went up river chose the straight path. He came to a bridge and crossed safely.

The man who went down river chose the meandering path and came to a point where he stopped believing in the bridge, because there was no bridge in this particular direction. He decided to swim across. Halfway across he was drowned.

When the man who went up river entered the Kingdom of Heaven, God asked him:

"Where are the others?"

And the man said:

"They drowned."

Then God said:

"Why did they not use the bridge?"

No.5

A masked man came to my door. I bid him enter and asked him his name. He said:
"My name is no matter."
I asked to see his face and he said:
"All you will see is death."
I said:
"How came you upon this burden?"
He said:
"I was walking the road to salvation and I came to a well. I drew water and filled my cup but it was a poisoned chalice."
I said:
"Pity the man who drinks from a poisoned chalice."
He said:
"It is pity that will save me yet."
I bid him sit and eat and he told me his full story:
"After I had drunk" he said, "I looked upon a face that was but an echo of love. I lost my heart and fell from grace and now I walk in shadow."
I said:
"Look not to the face but the heart."
He said:
"I am blind."
I said:
"Listen not for words of wisdom but for the steps of the faithful planted blind."
He said:

"Show me where to attach my hope."
I said:
"Cast all doubt aside and come empty handed."
He said:
"You speak the truth well yet I know not your name."
I said:
"It is written upon your heart."
With that the shadow fell from him and the answer to the question that bound his hands and feet had the strength to carry him where he could find no peace.
He removed his mask and I saw myself redeemed.

No.6

There was a man who loved the moon but it was beyond his command. One night he walked alone under the sky. The moon was full but his heart was empty. He came to a pool upon the road. In the pool he saw the moon and he was filled with joy but when he tried to gather it in his hands the water stirred and it disappeared. He did not understand for his love was true but he could not grasp it. It was a trial too sore for the human heart. So mortal was his wound that he took his own life.

When his spirit left his body the womb that bore him wept, leaving a pool of tears upon the road between life and death. He came to the pool of tears and in it saw the moon. Beyond mere reflection his eyes were opened and he cupped his hands to fill them. In his hands was the image of the moon. He held onto its promise and realised the love that he had touched upon in life. It brought him to a place where all was lost, save the love that he had touched.

No.7

Three men were walking from the womb to the tomb. They had been given a sack of provisions. They laid out the provisions and decided how best to divide the goods:

"Let us each choose something in turn" said the first man.

"Let me choose first for my journey is the more difficult" said the second man.

"Let me choose first for my journey is the more difficult" said the third man.

The second and third men drew lots to decide who should go first, whilst the first man was happy to go last. The matter was settled and all of them chose in turn, then the men went their separate ways.

When they met trouble on their journeys, the second and third men found that they did not have what they needed, whist the first man (who chose last) always had exactly what he needed.

No.8

A drowning man prayed to God for salvation. A ship found him but he refused its help because it carried a cargo of precious stones and his faith forbade the tender of precious stones.

He said:

"God will save me."

Then a second ship found him but he refused its help too because it carried a cargo of precious oils and his faith forbade the tender of precious oils.

He said:

"God will save me."

Despite being true to his faith the man drowned.

He found himself walking with God and he asked Him why his prayers had not been answered.

And God replied:

"I sent you two ships."

No.9

There were two leaders of two tribes who were enemies. One wanted freedom and the other wanted peace. For the sake of the children they sat down to talk. Concerned with love they spoke the truth.

The one for peace asked:

"What is freedom?"

And the one for freedom replied:

"A place of worship."

"Your daily life is your temple" said the one for peace.

The one for freedom asked:

"What is peace?"

And the one for peace replied:

"The fruit of love."

"Your fruit is in your root" said the one for freedom.

The one for peace said:

"Freedom needs an anchor."

The one for freedom said:

"Peace needs wings."

The one for peace said:

"Truth is an anchor."

The one for freedom said:

"Love is its wings."

The hunter gatherer emerged from his cave. The morning sun spread its wings of light and his spirit was released:
"I am here" it said.

He walked the path his father walked before him and in his father's steps he heard his father's voice:
"I am here" it said.

He entered the forest and gathered its fruits. He held them in his hands and said:
"I am here."

A wolf approached and looked him in the eye. He read the wolf's intentions but did not see death, for it was not his day to die but saw instead a kindred spirit in its eyes:
"I am here" it said.

A deer stirred and he speared it. The silence that followed its last heartbeat spoke to his heart:
"I am here" it said.

On his return he honoured the spoils in the fashion he was accustomed to, as he prepared his meal. The food was shared among his family and his spirit returned with a message from his creator:
"I am here."

The Last Supper

The bard belonged to no kingdom. He travelled through villages and towns singing his songs to anyone who would listen in exchange for a meal and a bed for the night. Weak and hungry he entered the city:

" Knock! Knock!" A woman came to the door. "Sweet bard you come at the right time" said the woman."This is the house of the merchant and today is our daughter's wedding day. If you sing a love song at the wedding feast you can sit with us at her table."

The bard stepped through the port-hole and in the farthest room in the house was a beautiful girl dressed in fine white satin. She wore a veil of white lace upon her head, with red ribbon woven into its delicate threads, covering her flaming hair. Red flowers had been plaited into the locks and curls loosely falling on either side of her flush rose-pink cheeks.

Deep within the bard's soul a song of love sang like a nightingale. Words flickered like flames and he harnessed them with rhyme. His breath fanned them as he spoke and they blossomed into flowers of fire that matched the girl's hair. His reason, as vital as the blood in his veins, bound his message like the red ribbon of her veil and shaped his heart into a beautiful bouquet.

Later that evening, after everyone had eaten, the bard was called to sing for the bride and groom his marriage song:
"To the bride: do not open your flower to the sun without opening your heart and do not bathe in his beauty without bathing in his love.

To the groom: do not drink from nature's cup without drinking from her heart and do not enter her temple without bringing your love.

Your children pick the fruits of your lives. Let love be their food and they will never hunger, even after you die."

When the bard had finished his marriage song the groom stood up and bowed before the bride's father. The bride shed a tear, as did her mother and everyone around the table was silent. The musicians started to play and one at a time men and women got up to dance. The father of the bride asked his wife to prepare a bed for the bard and that night he slept with an angel on his pillow.

The next morning he woke with a song in his heart and a prayer on his lips, he was given a good breakfast and went on his way:
"Knock! Knock!" A woman came to the door. "Sweet bard you come at the right time" said the woman. "This is the house of the City Treasurer and today he must speak to the people. If you can

write a speech for him you can sit at his table when the City Governor comes to hear him speak at the great ball tonight."

The bard stepped through the port-hole and in the farthest room in the house was a very wise man sitting at his desk. He wore a smart black suit with a black velvet ribbon tied in a bow around the stiff collar of his white shirt. The lamp on his desk gave light to where his wisdom was best applied.

Deep within the bard's soul a song for the people sang like a nightingale. Words fluttered like butterflies and in the light of new hopes he captured the shadow of one and pinned it with rhyme to match the shirt and tie of the Treasurer. The understanding with which he clothed his poetry was cut like the fine suit the Treasurer wore.

Later that evening, after everyone had eaten, the Treasurer was called to speak and with the words of the bard in his hands he sang a song for the people:

"The greatest treasure in the land" began the Treasurer, "is the heart of a man. The wealth of the nation is stored there. To receive this wealth we must open our hearts. To open our hearts we must be free.

A man's heart is the corner stone of the citadel and the citadel is the dominion to which our freedom is anchored. Its bricks are the souls of men and love is the mortar that binds them. If the mortar crumbles dominion is lost and freedom is crushed by falling bricks."

When the Treasurer had finished the song for the people, the Governor stood up and bowed before him. The Treasure's wife shed a tear, as did the Governor's and everyone around the table was silent. The musicians started to play and one at a time men and women got up to dance. The Treasurer asked his wife to prepare a bed for the bard and that night he slept with doves in his eyes.

The next morning he woke with a song in his heart and a prayer on his lips, he was given a good breakfast and went on his way:

"Knock! Knock!" A woman came to the door. "Sweet bard you come at the right time" said the woman. "Today the King is holding a feast for the poor. I shall fetch my husband the gate keeper and he will take you to the King. If you can sing a song at the feast you may sit at the King's table."

The bard stepped through the port-hole and in the farthest room in the palace was the King upon his throne. He wore a robe of white. His golden crown shone like the sun and in his hand he held a sceptre with a pearl as big as a fist clutched in a lion's claw. The King smiled upon the bard. Warming to his beautiful welcome the bard knelt down before the King:

"Forgive me my wretchedness great King" said the bard.

"Today all the poor are kings" replied the King.

Deep within the bard's soul a song for a king began to sing like a nightingale. Words of authority streamed out from the sunset of his soul. He took a golden sunbeam and forged it into a ring. He found a pearl of great price in the rising moon of his evening and placed it at the centre of the ring to match the King's sceptre and crown.

Later that evening, after everyone had eaten, the bard was called to sing his song for a king:
"From a beggar to a king" said the bard.

"The warrior wore a beggar's cloak,
  He had a weathered look.
  Upon his path there walked a king
  And where they met, they stood.

"I wish to pass"
  The warrior said.

"A beggar kneels before a king.
  Stand aside" was his answering.

"I wish to pass"
  The warrior said.

  The king he laughed instead
  And said:
"I go to the temple

For the nation's blessing -
I am a pilgrim king!"

The warrior spoke again:
"We walk this path
  From opposite ends,
  Upon such a path
  A man may tend
  To meet his soul
  My friend."

"Your friend?
  Your soul?
  Your path?"
  He laughed:
"Behind me is a throne
  Where only a king can go."

"I know" said the warrior
  Stepping aside.

"You dream" said the king
  Passing him by.

"My dream is your waking"
  The warrior said
  And the warrior shook his head.

From under his shroud
His hair unfolds
In lengths of flaming gold.
He bore a cross upon his breast
And his true strength now showed.

In the warrior's eyes
The king grew weak
And on the brink
The king did weep.

The king fell down
Upon his knees:
"I beg your pardon sire please!"
Said the king to the ground
Where the warrior stood
And he kissed the warrior's feet.

The warrior covered his glory again -
From beggar to king to beggar
He said:

"My heart is always open
And open may be broken.
I serve the King of love -
I am a warrior by God!"

The warrior walked on in faith
And the beggar king went with him.

From the temple to the capital
With a blessing for the nation."

When the bard had finished his song for a king the people all stood up and bowed before the King, as did the bard. There was not a tear in the house. Everyone around the table was silent. The musicians started to play and one at a time men and women got up to dance. The King asked the gatekeeper's wife to prepare a bed for the bard. As he was climbing the stairs the King said:
"Sweet bard I give you the freedom of the city, for this is the Kingdom of Heaven."
That night he slept with his soul in paradise:
"Knock! Knock!" A woman came to the door.
"Call the King" said a beggar to the gatekeeper's wife. So the King was called to the palace gates, where a small boy lay dead in the doorway of the gatehouse.
"What has happened?" said the King with great sadness and the beggar told the King about the boy's death:
"He entered the city three days ago" said the beggar, "I saw him go to the merchant's house but the merchant turned him away because his daughter was getting married that day. Then I saw him go to the Treasury and he was turned away from there too because the Treasurer was preparing for the great ball. Then he came to the palace but nobody

answered because you were busy ruling the nation."

"Who is he?" asked the King.

"He is the bard" replied the beggar.

   Then the King noticed that in the dead boy's hands were scrolls of paper.

"Let me see what he has written" he said and the beggar pushed the scrolls through the bars of the palace gates. First the King read the marriage song, then he read the song for the people, then he read the song for a king.

"This poor boy has reached deep into my soul" said the King, "he could not open this cage with his life but he has uncaged my heart with his death. Come let us bury him."

   The King lifted the boy up and carried him in his arms across the city to the Cathedral. All the King's people followed. When he got to the Cathedral he was met by the Arch Bishop.

"I'm carrying him to the catacombs to lay his body next to my father's" said the King and the Arch Bishop led the way. He laid the body in the space that was meant for himself. He knelt down and began to say a prayer:

"We cannot regain our innocence" he said "but this boy has restored my faith."

   In the echo of the catacombs the prayer was like words to a song and the sound of the song voiced its concern, to embrace the living with the same peace as is afforded the faithful dead.

The King placed the song for a king on the bard's chest and folded his hands across it then he handed the other two scrolls to the beggar saying: "Take these to the merchant and the Treasurer and tell them the good news - today our nation has restored its faith."

And the beggar went out to tell the good news.